4/98
4/9/97

DATE DUE

OCT 30 '68			

J   **Syme, Ronald**   31447 CL
B   Walter Raleigh   89
RAL   4-18-2002:
I.H.   C.C.Φ 2001
                                        INV

A short biography of Walter Raleigh who
became a favorite of Queen Elizabeth in
1581 and gave up his life of exploration to
become a part of her court. After her death
he was jailed for twelve years and executed
by King James on false charges. EHFVB

WALTER RALEIGH

Walter Raleigh

By RONALD SYME

Illustrated by WILLIAM STOBBS

WILLIAM MORROW AND COMPANY
New York   1962

*   *   *   *

Walter Raleigh was born in 1552 near Budleigh Salterton in Devonshire, six years before England's greatest Queen, the red-haired, shrewd, and hot-tempered Elizabeth the First, came to the throne at the age of twenty-five and united the country as never before.

The cultured splendor of the Elizabethan Age had dawned. The wealthy classes were taking a great new interest in all forms of learning. Craftsmen and artisans had become inspired with ambition to turn out works of art such as had never been seen before. This was also the England of great sea fighters and explorers, among them Sir Francis Drake. There were brilliant philosophers and statesmen, such as Francis Bacon; poets and dramatists, including Ben Jonson and the immortal Shakespeare himself. Talent and genius were blossoming throughout the whole of England.

But this bright splendor did not reach very far below the surface. Like all Europe of that time, England was still a barbarous country in many ways. Her fields and farms, forests and streams formed picturesque countrysides, but the towns lacked drainage and smelled abominable. Clever—or unscrupulous—men might acquire enormous and unlimited wealth for themselves, but a single slip could bring about their ruin. The torture rack and the execution block awaited those who were suspected of treason, or who even breathed a faint word of criticism against the Queen. There were judges and law courts, but a man's guilt or innocence usually depended on the size of his purse or the influence of his family. Private spies and agents—most of them utter villains—eagerly brought tittle-tattle to the Queen, but there was no such thing as a police force to protect the ordinary citizen. Life in those days was a dangerous gamble for any ambitious man.

Walter Raleigh was a born gambler. He knew that great prizes were to be won at Elizabeth's royal court in London, on a battlefield, or in newly discovered countries beyond the sea. He was still in his early teens when he determined to secure wealth and honor for himself.

At the age of sixteen he left Oxford University to become a soldier in a civil war in France. Military experience, he believed,

should be a part of every man's education.

The professors greatly lamented his departure. "Walter Raleigh was our most brilliant junior," they declared. "In another two years his great learning would have astounded all England."

But by that time Raleigh was a tired, mud-stained, and tattered soldier somewhere in France.

He came back to England in 1574. He was

quieter now, and his dark, gypsylike face had become hard. His whole bearing was cold, self-assured, and ruthless. The merciless war between the French Protestant Huguenots and the Catholics had made him bitter.

"One thing I have learned," he told his friends. "Civil war is an evil from which good can but seldom come. And when that war is brought on by religious differences, the results cause one to doubt the benefits of Christianity."

Raleigh decided that the next subject he should know something about was law. He began studying in London, but became extremely bored. He was not a person to stand boredom for long. It made him dangerous.

"I pray you to be silent," he said one evening to a tiresome acquaintance, whose voice droned on endlessly, "like a drum in the room."

The foolish young man paid no attention

to Raleigh's request. After a surprised pause, he went on prating.

Raleigh leaped on him like an enraged tiger. Within a few seconds he had closed the fellow's mouth by fastening his mustache to his beard with sealing wax.

Soon afterward he challenged another student to a sword duel. Much to his opponent's relief—for Raleigh was a superb swordsman—they were both arrested by a party of soldiers just as they had drawn their blades. Raleigh was sentenced to seven days' imprisonment, and spent it in London's filthy and overcrowded Fleet Prison. After that he gave up trying to study law, and went back to his home in Devonshire. There the sea and the boats brought him pleasure and contentment.

Raleigh's family included many distinguished soldiers and sea fighters. One of them was Sir Humphrey Gilbert, his own half brother. Sir Humphrey was a tall, eagle-faced

man with gracious manners, unlimited ambition, and the reputation of being a merciless soldier. For years he had been asking the English government's permission to found a large-scale settlement in North America. Most of Gilbert's schemes were too ambitious and costly. Now, with Raleigh's shrewd advice, he submitted a more modest plan. He desired leave to take a mere one hundred settlers to "the northern part of America . . . inhabited by a savage people of a mild but tractable disposition. This is of all unfrequented places the one most fitted and most commodious for us to meddle with."

The request was granted. Apart from Florida, where some Frenchmen had attempted to settle, North America was still a land of mystery. A spell seemed to hang over that wild, vast continent across the Atlantic Ocean. Like all the early explorers, Gilbert and Raleigh believed North America to be a kind

12

of earthly Eden, conveniently filled with gold.

Gilbert's expedition sailed in November, 1578. With it went Walter Raleigh, bound for adventure. The hostile warships of Spain sighted the English vessels at sea and opened fire. Gilbert's largest ship was 150 tons and carried only 12 small guns. The Spanish warships were three times bigger and mounted forty, fifty, and sixty cannon. The little English fleet was forced to escape. Walter Raleigh found himself back in England without having even sighted the New World. He was twenty-seven years old, and his first attempt to earn fame and fortune for himself had failed. All he had gained was a bitter and undying hatred of Spain.

Sixty miles across the sea from England, Ireland was in a state of rebellion. The ragged, wild, and poverty-stricken Irish were trying to drive the overbearing English colonists out of their country. Small companies of Spanish and Italian troops, who had landed secretly on the lonely rocky coasts, were helping them.

Queen Elizabeth was out to suppress the rebellion, but it was easier said than done. The Irish were desperate fighters in the bogs and mountains of their native country, and more and more British troops had to be sent from England.

"Now here lies a fair chance for me to

catch Her Majesty's eye," Raleigh said to a friend. "Any man who distinguishes himself in the royal service can expect to be rewarded. Our Queen is as generous in her rewards as she is harsh in her punishments."

Raleigh sailed for Ireland as captain of a company of infantry. The only warfare he knew was the merciless kind he had learned in France. Now he practiced it in Ireland. No quarter was given on the battlefield, and death was the punishment of all rebels wherever they were caught.

At least he established a reputation for bravery. Once when he was crossing a shallow river with one soldier as companion, a crowd of Irish rebels burst out from a clump of willows and attacked them. Raleigh broke clear and reached the farther bank. There he saw that the soldier had been thrown from his horse and was struggling in midstream against twenty attackers. Raleigh turned back at once

to help the man. He held off the ambushers with his sword until his men arrived.

The governor of Ireland at that time was Lord Grey. He was a weak and muddle-headed man. Raleigh, who could never learn to be patient with fools, soon quarreled with him. Lord Grey went off in a temper to complain to the Queen. Raleigh followed him. They met on the spacious oak floor of a vast crowded audience hall in the royal palace, where Queen Elizabeth reposed on a richly canopied throne.

Lord Grey burst into a peevish, vague, and overlong statement regarding the Irish rebellion. He went on to blame Raleigh for disobedience. Elizabeth, none too tolerant of fools herself, listened with impatience.

At last the Queen's hard blue eyes glanced curiously at Walter Raleigh, whose face now wore an expression of polite boredom. This was the first time Elizabeth had seen him.

"And you, Master Raleigh," she said curtly. "What have you to say in answer to the hard words our good Lord Grey has spoken about Ireland and yourself?"

"That if I thrust my hand into a bag containing wildcats, Your Majesty, I would expect to be badly scratched," Raleigh replied humorously. "Moreover, I would find it hard to seize one of those cats and bring it forth."

A faint smile appeared on the Queen's imperious face. "I follow your meaning, Master Raleigh," she said, speaking clearly in the silent hall, where everyone was listening eagerly. "You may continue."

"I," went on Raleigh, bowing toward the throne, "would sooner turn those cats loose, and provide them regularly with food and all the liberty they needed. They would be free to continue fighting among themselves if they wished. But the day would surely come when the wiser cats would no longer want to claw the hand of him who fed them. They might even turn and rend any of their own kind who wished to do so."

The Queen studied Raleigh carefully. Her shrewd mind was busy interpreting his remarks. "Make peace with the Irish rebel leaders who are willing," she translated. "Then leave them to pacify—or destroy—those other leaders who wish to continue war against us. It is a clever thought, Master Raleigh. I trust it is one that our good Lord Grey will remember."

Thus did Queen Elizabeth and Raleigh begin their long friendship. "For," wrote an old historian, "Walter Raleigh had much the better in the telling of his tale, and the Queen and the Lords took no small notice of him and the words he uttered."

At the age of twenty-nine, Raleigh had at last set his feet on the wide but dangerous road that led to fame.

To the noble stone-walled Whitehall Palace in London, where Elizabeth spent most of her time, came all kinds of men. Proud and arrogant courtiers in velvet and lace thronged the spacious corridors on their way to and from the great audience hall. With them came pensive men of learning, threadbare adventurers in hungry need of royal assistance, black-bearded, haughty foreign

ambassadors and their fussy secretaries, richly robed ladies of the aristocracy, and persons of great family and name. There were also many humble people, whom no one knew by name or sight, but who had come to seek some small favor or to beg the Queen's assistance to right a wrong.

Above the audience hall and the other spacious chambers was the private royal suite, where the public never intruded. Here the

Queen spoke with her intimate friends and advisers, held formal dinner parties, and met with those who came by night on secret business to whisper confidential reports.

Like any other person, Queen Elizabeth had her favorites, to whom she granted the right of admittance to the royal suite. Among them were William Cecil, Lord Burleigh, a famous statesman, and the forty-nine-year-old Robert Dudley, Earl of Leicester. Dudley had grown up with Elizabeth, and was her closest friend. It was whispered throughout England, though, that he had murdered his wife, Amy Robsart, two years after Elizabeth came to the throne. None dared say so openly, however. Such talk would cost them their lives.

Sir Christopher Hatton was also allowed in the royal suite. He was a rather silly little man, who had endeared himself to the Queen by his skill in dancing. Unkind courtiers described him as "a mere vegetable of the court that sprang up at night."

In 1582, a newcomer was admitted to this circle of intimate friends. Big solidly built Walter Raleigh seemed to bring a welcome touch of fresh country air and sunshine to the stuffy, overfurnished rooms. He met curious glances coolly, spoke briefly to those who tried to fuss over him, ignored Christopher Hatton's perturbed squeaks of jealousy, and let it be clearly seen that he towered above the

others as much in mind as he did in body. He never troubled to lose the broad country accent of his native Devon. Perhaps he knew that Elizabeth delighted in listening to the soft, attractive dialect. As long as the Queen befriended him, he could ignore the scores, even hundreds, of jealous enemies who were already gathering against him.

Five years after the Queen had first set eyes on him, thirty-four-year-old Raleigh had

been awarded a knighthood and various
official appointments. His yearly income
amounted to $300,000. Elizabeth had also
given him a handsome London mansion,
staffed by forty servants, a vast country estate,
and 40,000 acres of land in Ireland. The
beautiful poetry he was composing also
brought him honor among the cultured classes
of England.

But Raleigh was not content with his life

at court. The blood of adventurous, seafaring ancestors ran strongly in his veins. He yearned to exchange the stuffy, over-perfumed, and doubtful air of Whitehall Palace for the keen breezes and salt spray of the ocean. Instead of soft rugs and polished floors, he wished to feel the salty deck of a ship beneath his feet once more.

But he was no longer free to please himself. The Queen expected much in exchange for the wealth she had given him. The older Elizabeth grew, the more she liked to keep her favorites close to the palace.

"I wish I were in your place, Walter," Sir Humphrey Gilbert once said to Raleigh, after he had recently returned from another voyage of exploration.

"By Heaven, I wish you *were*," Raleigh replied impulsively. "Then *I* would be the one to sail the western ocean. I would eat and drink aboard a ship with greater appetite than I can show for the fancy dishes set before me here in London."

Raleigh financed another voyage for his half brother in the year 1583. It was the nearest he could get to adventure for himself.

Gilbert's five little ships reached the black, icebound coasts of Newfoundland, and then bore onward in search of the fabled Northwest Passage, which would lead to the riches of China and the East Indies. Only two ships, the *Squirrel* and the *Golden Hind,* survived to begin the homeward voyage to England. A gale met them in mid-Atlantic. The captain of the larger *Golden Hind* implored Gilbert to leave the little *Squirrel,* and find safety in the bigger ship.

"I will not forsake my little company going homeward. I have passed many storms and perils with them," Gilbert replied.

He stayed aboard the *Squirrel.*

"The same Monday night," wrote a sailor

on the *Golden Hind,* "about twelve of the clock, the frigate *(Squirrel)* being ahead of us, suddenly her lights went out . . . and our watch cried the General was cast away, which was too true. For in that moment the frigate was devoured and swallowed up by the sea."

Raleigh grieved deeply for poor Gilbert, but he would not give up his dream of colonizing North America. "It would be a noble work to carry on the cause for which Sir Humphrey died," he suggested to the Queen. "A thriving English colony would make a fitting monument to his memory."

"Plague take it!" exlaimed Elizabeth, who used strong expressions. "Who can pay the cost of another expedition across the ocean? Spain threatens this little country of ours increasingly day by day. The money of our treasury must go to the building of warships and the casting of cannon with which to arm them."

"Then I ask leave to meet the costs of such an expedition myself, Your Majesty," Raleigh replied coolly.

"Your hatband of pearls and your diamond earrings should raise a pretty sum when you dispose of them," Elizabeth said peevishly.

Raleigh bowed. "Should I have to dispose of such trinkets, then I will beg leave to remain at my country home. I would not dare to give offense by appearing half-dressed in front of England's Queen."

Elizabeth, who dearly loved bargaining, gave way to him. "Build your ships and choose your men," she ordered. "I pray you not to sell the clothes from your back. The money will be found."

Another little expedition sailed for the New World in April, 1585. Once again the Queen refused to allow Raleigh to go. In command of the expedition was forty-three-year-old Sir Richard Grenville, a sea captain noted for his cold and reckless courage. He was one of Raleigh's first cousins from Devonshire.

The ships reached Roanoke Island off the coast of what is now North Carolina. The 107 new settlers failed to make a success of their little colony. They had been selected badly. There were too many tailors and too few ploughmen, too many adventurous gentlemen and not enough blacksmiths and farmers. Sir Francis Drake, returning from a plundering raid on the Spanish Main, called at Roanoke Island in 1586. At the colonists' own urgent request, he brought them all back to England in his ships.

But Raleigh remained unbeaten. He was determined that English colonies should be established in America. Next year he tried again. Another 150 colonists sailed for Virginia in 1587. Their fate is a mystery. When the next English ship called at Roanoke Island, there was no sign of the settlers. They

had simply disappeared, and their log cabins lay in ruins. No doubt they were massacred by the Indians.

So ended Raleigh's first attempts to found a colony overseas. Although Elizabeth had helped him financially to some extent, he had spent a fortune of his own. Raleigh may have been ruthless and greedy for gold, but at least he was a greater pioneer and statesman than those who surrounded him at court. As far as others were concerned, the Indians were welcome to keep North America for as long as they chose. Or if the Indians failed to keep intruders out, the Dutch, French, and Spanish could claim the country.

Among the colonists who came home with Drake in 1586 was a young man named Thomas Harriot, who was one of Raleigh's closest friends. Harriot, who had been a poor student until Raleigh befriended him, was a brilliant mathematician, scientist, and astronomer. He had gone to Virginia at Raleigh's request.

"Be my eyes and ears across the ocean," Raleigh had said to him. "Write down all that I should know about this country we have named Virginia."

Harriot carried out his orders faithfully. *A Brief and True Report of the Land of Virginia* was the best travel book that had ever appeared in England. It dealt with agriculture, plants, minerals, the Indians, climate, and types of fish in rivers and sea. Among other matters it described the use of tobacco by the Indians. As the returning colonists had brought a quantity of tobacco with them, Raleigh tried smoking. He enjoyed it so much that he encouraged the people of England to adopt the habit. In this way he was responsible for introducing tobacco to Europe.

"I understand tobacco so well, Your Majesty," he said to Queen Elizabeth, when she laughed at his long clay pipe, "that I can even tell how much the smoke weighs."

"And I will wager you, Sir Walter," Elizabeth replied, "that no man alive could do that."

Raleigh, who was already becoming a skilled scientist under Harriot's tuition, carefully weighed a quantity of tobacco, and smoked it. He collected the ash from his pipe and weighed that. The difference between the two weights, he alleged, was the weight of the smoke.

The Queen paid up. "I have heard of many people who turned their gold into smoke," she said, "but you are the first man I have seen turn smoke into gold."

In 1587, Raleigh began to share Elizabeth's friendship with a younger man who had recently appeared at Whitehall Palace.

Robert Devereux, Earl of Essex, was a mem-

ber of the great nobility of England. He was nearly as tall as Raleigh, only twenty-one years old, handsome, vain, and recklessly bold toward the aging Queen.

The two men disliked each other from the start. Essex let it be known that he regarded Raleigh as a man of inferior family. But Essex, who was a muddler, was jealous of Raleigh's reputation as a brilliantly clever man and as one of England's leading poets. When Lord Burleigh and Raleigh spoke together on matters of state, Essex could scarcely understand their conversation. Whenever Essex made a jest, Raleigh immediately, without hesitation, capped it with another one that was far wittier.

Raleigh disliked Essex, whom he regarded as a scatterbrained young man, with little but a handsome face and elegant manners to recommend him. It continually annoyed him that the Queen had so much time to spare for

Essex. Lord Burleigh was inclined to agree with Raleigh; it had come to his knowledge that Essex called him "the old fox" behind his back.

During the next thirteen years Raleigh and Essex remained like cat and dog. Only Elizabeth could keep the peace between them. The people of England preferred Essex to Raleigh. Only toward the end did they begin to realize who was the better man.

In the year 1588, a great danger threatened England from across the sea. King Philip of Spain, England's bitter enemy, had decided to launch a great invasion force and conquer the country. There was no doubt that he had the ships and men with which to carry out his plans.

Spies brought news of the Spanish plans to England. Elizabeth turned to her grim professional soldiers and seamen for advice and guidance. Among these advisers was the hard-faced Raleigh, bitter in his hatred against Spain.

"Spanish troops fight well enough on land," these veterans of war told Elizabeth, "but the Spaniards are an unhandy nation afloat. Being afraid of the sea, they build great unwieldy ships, which resemble the Biblical ark. They despise the gun as an invention of cowards, who do not dare fight hand to hand. We should engage the Spanish fleet with gunfire, but never, never at close quarters. Our sailors would find it hard to climb aboard a vessel twice the height of their own, and defended by four or five times their own numbers. Let our own little ships worry the great enemy galleons as hounds worry a cornered wild boar."

The Spanish Armada, or fleet of warships, was sighted off the coast of southern England on July 20, 1588. The 134 great ships were lumbering in an easterly direction toward the mouth of the Thames River and London. There the Earl of Leicester was awaiting their arrival with a grim and compact little army. Aboard the Spanish vessels were 18,000 soldiers and 8000 sailors.

Out to meet the Spanish fleet sailed Elizabeth's 34 warships. They were low-decked, black-hulled, and dangerous little vessels, which could spray a crowded deck with grape-shot—150 musket balls packed into each charge. Astern of these ships came 50 privately owned merchant vessels, which now mounted guns and carried veteran gunners. Among them went the big *Ark Raleigh* and the little powder-carrying *Roebuck,* both vessels belonging to Raleigh himself. Aboard these 84 ships were 9000 sailors. There were no soldiers.

As the first rumble of gunfire rolled shoreward across the summer sea, Raleigh went quickly to the palace. "I pray Your Majesty

to allow me to sail against the Dons," he pleaded. "How can I remain ashore while my own ship engages the enemy?"

But even now Elizabeth would not allow Raleigh to go. "I have entrusted you to see that our ships remain well supplied," she answered. "The battle may be long. Our seamen will need more gunpowder and shot, water and food. It is more important that you remain ashore to make sure those needs are fully met."

British gunfire shot the Spanish fleet to pieces, as the battle rolled eastward across the sea. At last the battered Armada tried to flee back to Spain by sailing round the northern end of Scotland. A northwesterly storm overwhelmed their shot-ripped hulls and shattered rigging. Many of the cumbersome vessels were driven onto the unfriendly shores of Scotland and Ireland, where their unfortunate crews were murdered by the savage peasants. Only

fifty of the Spanish ships ever returned to Cadiz.

"And many of them who came home," wrote a historian, "by reason of the toils and inconveniences which they had sustained in this voyage, died not long after their arrival."

Once the fear of invasion was over, the English Court was free to return to its petty squabbling and minor jealousies. Raleigh was growing more tired than ever of the useless life he was forced to lead. He yearned to board a ship and sail away to some far-off country in search of adventure. But now he was kept closer than ever to the throne. Young Essex had just married secretly. When Elizabeth learned of it, she was furious, and had him banished from court. Now she turned back to her trusted Raleigh for friendship.

But at least Raleigh was able to interest himself in the adventures of others on the high seas. England and Spain still remained at war with one another. Spain's great wealth from the gold and silver mines of Peru flowed homeward each year in galleons bound from Panama to Cadiz.

"The swiftest way to hurt Spain is to empty her pockets," Raleigh told the Queen, in the privacy of her oak-paneled study. "A few well-armed English ships, patrolling the sea approaches to Spain, might bring Your Majesty great profit."

The Queen was by no means displeased. "Why is it that all you gentlemen of Devon have the cunning of a highwayman and a pirate's greed for gold?"

"Because we are always the first to find a profitable way to help Your Majesty against her enemies," Raleigh replied smoothly.

The Queen studied his dark and neatly bearded face. "I know you well, Sir Walter," she murmured. "Therefore, I ask, what share of booty will be mine?"

"Enough to make Your Majesty well content," Raleigh replied, with a courteous bow.

The Queen nodded. "Send out the ships," she commanded. "Be sure I find no cause for complaint in the division of the spoils."

Raleigh's privateering ships met with misfortune at the start. In that year of 1591, they sighted the homeward-bound Spanish treasure fleet off the Azores, a group of islands in mid-Atlantic. But what Raleigh's sea captains did not see in time was that the treasure-carrying galleons were being escorted by 53 Spanish warships. The privateers were forced to flee. Raleigh's cousin, the recklessly wild Sir Richard Grenville, covered their flight with his own ship, the 500-ton *Revenge*.

So began one of England's most famous sea battles. For 15 hours the 200 men of the *Revenge* successfully fought off the 53 Spanish ships. They killed 800 of the enemy, sank 2 vessels, and smashed 8 others. With ammunition gone, and reduced to a mastless, blazing, and sinking wreck, the *Revenge* was at last boarded by the Spaniards. Sir Richard Grenville and more than half his crew died during the action.

Raleigh sent out more privateers from England. They brought home booty worth $200,000 within a few months. In January, 1592, Elizabeth gratefully presented him with Sherborne Castle, a beautiful country resi-

dence, which became his beloved home until almost the end of his life.

And then Raleigh made an incautious mistake. Elizabeth Throckmorton was one of the Queen's maids of honor. She was a quiet, pretty, and intelligent girl. But Raleigh married her in secret, and that, to the Queen, was an insult. First Robert, Earl of Essex, and now Sir Walter Raleigh had married without making his intentions known beforehand.

Raleigh was arrested and imprisoned in the grim, stone-walled Tower of London beside the Thames River.

His privateers, roving the high seas, brought his release within a few months. Off the Azores they captured the great *Madre de Dios,* a galleon homeward bound to Spain with a cargo of rare and costly spices, diamonds, pearls, and silk.

The captured ship was brought into Dartmouth harbor in Devonshire, which was Raleigh's own county. The people there were indignant at his arrest and sorry for his young wife. This resentment had made them bitter against the Queen.

"She's put our Walter Raleigh in the Tower; now we'll put her wealth in our pockets," they grumbled.

Dangerous crowds of sturdy fishermen, sailors, and laborers, descended on the *Madre de Dios* where she lay, anchored against the quay.

They broke open treasure chests and barrels, looted sacks of cinnamon worth $300 each, and crammed their pockets with valuables. Goldsmiths and merchants rushed westward from London to buy this loot. One sailor sold "a chain of orient pearls, two chains of gold, four great pearls of the bigness of a fair pea, four forks of crystal, and four spoons of crystal, set with gold and stones."

The Queen's men were unable to stop the looting. Bared knife blades and threatening clubs drove them away from the ship. Twenty-eight-year-old Robert Cecil, the hunchback son of Lord Burleigh, was sent by the Queen to restore order.

He failed to control the mob and sent a frantic message to the Queen. "Only Sir Walter Raleigh can control these wild and willful people. Were he released from prison he might come here speedily."

Elizabeth, who saw a fortune vanishing be-

fore her greedy eyes, rushed the order for Raleigh's release. He rode to Dartmouth as swiftly as possible. When he appeared on the quay, a roar of welcome greeted him. Order was restored and looting ceased. Even though much of the cargo from the *Madre de Dios* had disappeared by that time, it still took ten English ships to carry the rest of it from Dartmouth to London.

This time it was Elizabeth who had won the bargain. She got half the wealth from the *Madre de Dios*. Raleigh got nothing except his freedom.

For five years after that he was not allowed to appear at Whitehall Palace. Perhaps it was not as heavy a punishment as the Queen believed. Raleigh and his wife lived peacefully at lovely Sherborne Castle, and their son Walter was born there in 1594. They laid out the handsome grounds, and planted the good clay soil with graceful trees from the tropics,

bright flowers from the West Indies, and fragrant cedars from Virginia. This was perhaps the most peaceful and happy period of Raleigh's stormy life.

He still took a great interest in everything to do with the New World. One peculiar story fascinated his imagination, and it is strange that a hard-bitten person like Raleigh could have believed its foolish and fantastic nonsense.

It was said that the Incas, driven out of Peru by the Spanish conquerors, had built a new and splendid city for themselves in the wilds of South America. And comparatively modern explorers agree that it is quite possible some of the Inca nobility did escape from Peru to found a small settlement of their own somewhere in the interior of South America. The name of this city was Manoa, and it was supposed to stand beside a Lake Parima, somewhere in Venezuela. A captive

Spanish officer, Juan Martinez, was said to have been taken to this city by the natives. He declared that Manoa was so vast that the distance from the outer walls to the emperor's palace was twenty miles. In the palace itself the last of the Inca nobility, clad in fine robes and bedecked with priceless jewelry, still lived with all their customary barbaric splendor.

Martinez was perhaps the most fertile and convincing liar the world has ever known. The story he told, which spread all over Europe, ended by declaring that although Martinez had filled his pockets with jewels before leaving Manoa, he had lost the lot when his canoe overturned! Thus the only proof of his story was missing.

"I pray you to find some way to draw my husband back to London," a worried Lady Raleigh wrote to kindly old Lord Burleigh, "for should he not so be drawn, he will set forth toward the sunset on a voyage of much peril. And this I pray, if any respect for me or love for Sir Walter be not forgotten."

The Queen, who was growing increasingly shrewish with age, was not yet in a forgiving mood. But at least she gave Raleigh permission to set forth on his proposed voyage of discovery.

"A galleon filled with gold once bought my freedom," Raleigh said to his friend Harriot. "What could I not gain if I discovered a golden empire for our Queen?"

According to Martinez, Manoa lay in the heart of a pleasant country which was situated several hundred miles to the south of the Orinoco River. In March, 1595, forty-three-year-old Raleigh landed in Trinidad from the little fleet of ships, which he himself had financed. He attacked the Spanish fort, which stood on that island, and captured it easily. Then he prepared to lead his men southward to the Orinoco River.

A narrow and dangerous channel, known as the Serpent's Mouth, divided Trinidad from the mainland of South America. Down this strait went Raleigh and his hundred companions, traveling in five heavy-timbered open boats. It was a terrible voyage. Wrote Raleigh:

We were all driven to lie in the rain and weather. In the open air, the burning sun, and upon the hard boards . . . and what with the victuals being most fish, with wet clothes of so many men thrust together, and the heat of the sun, I will undertake there was never any prison in England that could be found more loathsome.

Conditions became worse the farther they went. They were only 8° north of the equator, and the heat was so intense that many of the men suffered from sunstroke.

When three days more were overgone,
our companies began to despair, the weather being extreme hot, the river being bor-
dered with the very high trees that kept
away the air, and the current against us
every day stronger than the day before.

Raleigh encouraged his men to keep tugging
at the oars. On the fifteenth day after leaving
the ships, he believed that at last they were

drawing near to the frontiers of the mysterious kingdom of Manoa.

On both sides of the river we passed the most beautiful country that mine eyes ever beheld . . . the grass short and green and in many places groves of trees by themselves . . . and still, as we rowed, the deer came down feeding by the waterside as if they had been used to a keeper's call.

Indians met the expedition in this fine open country. They brought with them pork, venison, chicken, fish, and coconuts. Raleigh's hungry men filled their stomachs, and grew merry on the strong fermented juice of pineapples.

"Stay with us and become our king," the Indians pleaded with Raleigh. "Only the Spaniards have passed through this country before you, and them we hate for their cruelty and greed. You could protect us from their wickedness."

The Orinoco River defeated Raleigh. Tropical rain began falling, and the river started rising at such a rate that his boats could make no headway against it. He gave the order to begin the return journey to Trinidad. In August, 1595, his ships finally reached England.

Poor Raleigh! He left more gold in this

fever-laden country than he ever brought away from it. He had given many of the Indians pieces of "the new money of twenty shillings with Her Majesty's picture." It would have been better for him if he had left Guiana, which was the Indian name for that region, forever to the sun.

Those cool highland prairies of the Orinoco remained a vision to Raleigh for the rest of his life. He longed to see them settled by English colonists, and wrote a book, entitled *Discovery of the Large, Rich, and Beautiful Empire of Guiana,* about them. The book was a best seller. Shakespeare, who was inclined to show jealousy of Raleigh's many accomplishments, was deeply affected by reading it. He included some of the fanciful legends it contained in *The Tempest* and *Othello.*

But Raleigh was too far ahead of his time. England was not yet interested in establishing colonies in the New World. Not until another twelve years had passed did the first colony of Virginia come into existence.

By 1596, Elizabeth had recovered from her anger against Essex and Raleigh. Both were restored to favor. The Queen had need of all the military leaders she could get at that time. The war with Spain still dragged on, and the people of England were beginning to complain about its cost.

"Now is the time to give Spain a blow to the heart," Elizabeth's advisers suggested. "Let us attack her chief port, Cadiz, and capture the entire treasure fleet of Spain. It would be an injury from which that country would never recover."

Elizabeth agreed. Both Raleigh and Essex were among the leaders of the expedition. Ninety-six English ships and 14,000 men arrived off Cadiz on June 22, 1596. Essex, who was in command of the troops and impatient

to distinguish himself in action ashore, ordered his men into the boats. The sea was rough, and half a gale was blowing. The boats were capsized and men drowned. The whole attack on Cadiz became a hopeless muddle. In desperation, old Lord Howard, the supreme commander, appealed to Raleigh to take charge.

"Then we attack by sea," said Raleigh. "Keep the troops aboard."

Next morning he led the ships into the harbor, their guns firing destructive broadsides. Raleigh made straight for the mighty *San Pablo*, the warship that had played the chief part in the sinking of the *Revenge* and the death of his cousin, Sir Richard Grenville. Within an hour the *San Pablo* was a deserted, sinking, and blazing ruin. Raleigh had paid off an old score.

"Now land your troops," Raleigh told Essex, and the infantry swept forward from the wharves to capture the city.

A stray shot smashed Raleigh's right leg. He ordered his seamen to carry him ashore, and even tried to mount a horse. But the pain and loss of blood were too great. He had to be taken back aboard his ship. Meanwhile, Essex lost control of his troops ashore, and the Spanish leaders saw their chance. They set fire to their anchored treasure ships and destroyed them all. England lost $12,000,000 in the flames.

After this expedition returned to England, men began looking at Sir Walter Raleigh in a different way. Till now they had regarded him as a selfish, self-centered person, much too clever for their liking. But now the whole story of the Cadiz expedition had come out. It was very clear to everyone that Essex, the spoiled young man, had nearly wrecked it. Raleigh alone had saved the situation, and

he modestly kept quiet about the part he had played. Public opinion changed overnight. From then on, his popularity in England began to increase rapidly. One of Raleigh's bitter-tongued enemies at court made a handsome confession. "I never knew the gentleman until this time, and I am sorry for it, for there are in him excellent things besides his valor."

The Queen's attitude also changed. By 1597, Raleigh was once again her favorite friend. But the following year Lord Burleigh died, and his son, now Sir Robert Cecil, became Elizabeth's chief adviser.

"Dwarf Cecil," as he was known, was thirty-three years old. His clever mind was as crooked as his misshapen body. Past friendships meant nothing to him. The horrid little creature set out coolly to destroy both Essex and Raleigh—not together, he decided, but one at a time. The younger and much less clever Essex must be the first to go.

Essex made matters easy for him. Cecil arranged for Essex to be sent to Ireland, where a fresh rebellion had broken out. He knew that Essex was as useless a leader on the battlefield as he was a handsome ornament at court.

Essex wasted men, money, and time in chasing the elusive Irish across the country. Finally he broke Elizabeth's direct orders and made a shameful peace with the Irish rebel leader, Tyrone. He returned to London to tell the Queen what he had done. But Elizabeth already knew. Cecil had very carefully seen to that.

"What are you doing here, my lord?" the Queen exclaimed, when Essex strode into her study, fresh from the sweating horse on which he had galloped to the palace. "Your presence is hateful without Tyrone's head. I pray you leave immediately. Your boots do stink most unpleasantly."

Essex tried to argue. The Queen promptly smacked his face.

Essex was arrested that evening. He was soon freed, but now he was banished from court. Half crazy with fury, he suspected that his misfortune had been caused by Raleigh and Cecil, and at least he was right about the latter.

Mustering the soldiers who had gone with him to Ireland, Essex set about organizing a

rebellion "to free the Queen of her evil coun-
selors."

Cecil soon learned about the plot. He had
plenty of private spies, led by a man called
Waad, one of the nastiest villains in English
history. Essex's rebellion was a disastrous fail-
ure. Once again he was arrested and taken to
the Tower of London. This time there was no
royal forgiveness for him. The Queen, as it is
said, may have wept when she signed his
death warrant, but nevertheless she signed it.
On February 25, 1601, thirty-four-year-old
Essex, handsome and unafraid to the last,
died on the scaffold.

It had all turned out just as "dwarf Cecil"
had planned. Shuffling back to his den, with
its heavily curtained windows, angled mir-
rors, and secret entrances, he now set about
destroying Raleigh.

It is one of the mysteries of history why
Cecil hated Raleigh. Raleigh had never done

him any harm; in fact, he had done him several good turns. Cecil's son, Will, a delicate boy, spent long vacations as the guest of Raleigh and his wife at lovely Sherborne Castle. They treated the boy as if he were their own son, and he loved them both in return. No quarrel had ever occurred between Cecil and Raleigh.

Perhaps Cecil was jealous of Raleigh's tall figure and handsome appearance. Perhaps he could not bear a man who was so many things that he himself was not. He may have been insanely jealous of Raleigh's genius as a poet, soldier, and sailor, scientist, explorer, and statesman. One can only guess at the dark, unpleasant thoughts in the little man's mind.

The seventy-year-old Elizabeth died on March 24, 1603. The strange friendship between the Queen and Raleigh, which had lasted for twenty-one years, was ended. As

long as Elizabeth had remained alive, Cecil
did not dare to meddle openly with Raleigh
for fear of the royal fury. Now Raleigh stood
alone. The splendor of the Elizabethan Age
was fading. Indeed, he was almost the last
great Elizabethan still left alive.

The new king of England was James the
First. This shambling, deceitful man was born
in Scotland. His mother was Mary Stuart, a
willful Scottish queen; his father was a weak

and worthless man named Lord Darnley. It was probably Mary Stuart who gave the order for the house in which Darnley slept to be blown up with gunpowder. She had grown tired of her useless husband. Mary herself was afterwards beheaded in England by Elizabeth for plotting to seize the English throne.

James was a worthy son of such parents. The French king described him as "the wisest fool in Christendom." He was well-educated but utterly conceited. He never believed he could be wrong and other people right. In his treatment of Raleigh he was soon to show himself to be a thorough renegade. This was the man whom Cecil had schemed and plotted to have crowned king of England. They made a pretty pair.

Now Cecil moved fast. On July 14, 1603, Raleigh was arrested on a charge of plotting against King James. No one could have blamed him for doing so, but there was absolutely no worthwhile evidence that he had.

Legal justice did not exist in those times. Every official connected with the court was crooked. Raleigh was not allowed to have a lawyer to defend him. He was not allowed to cross-examine witnesses. He did not even know what charge was to be made against him until he appeared in court. Popham, the judge, was a former highwayman. Coke, the prosecuting attorney, was a rogue who took bribes and who usually falsified evidence to suit himself. It is said he was the greatest scoundrel who ever practiced law in England.

Raleigh, lame and gray-haired now, held his own against these human jackals in court. He proved to be a great deal more quick-witted than Coke.

Coke: I want words sufficient to express thy viperous treason.

Raleigh: I think you want words indeed, for you have spoken one thing half a dozen times.

Coke: Thou art an odious fellow. Thy name is hateful to all the realm of England for thy pride.

Raleigh: It will go near to a measuring cast between you and me, Mr. Attorney.

In any modern court Raleigh would have been quickly discharged as not guilty for lack of evidence. But in that English court of 1603 he was found guilty and condemned to death by beheading.

But now the people of England began muttering angrily among themselves. They remembered that Raleigh had helped to smash the Spanish Armada. Veteran soldiers and sailors recalled how he alone had led them to victory at Cadiz. Poets, philosophers, and playwrights spoke loudly of the beauty of Raleigh's poetry and the brilliance of his mind.

James feared the English people as much as they despised him. Cecil realized that he himself had gone too far. Raleigh's sentence of death was commuted. He was sentenced to imprisonment for life in the Tower of London.

Raleigh spent twelve years in prison. During that time James and Cecil schemed to ruin him financially. They succeeded perfectly. Raleigh's yearly income was reduced to $1200, and his wife and child were compelled to live on poor Lady Raleigh's own small income. The King then went on to retake possession of Sherborne Castle. A greedy and envious man, he could keep his hands off nothing that he wanted for himself.

During those years in the Tower, Raleigh built himself a tiny laboratory. There he discovered the medicinal use of quinine, invent-

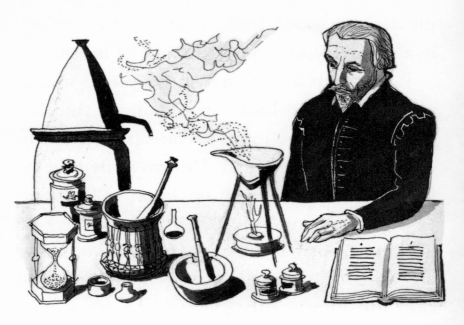

ed a clever new method of obtaining fresh water from salt water, developed a scientific method of curing tobacco, and experimented with all kinds of hitherto unknown chemical substances.

King James's fifteen-year-old son, Henry, was very different from his royal father. It was already being said in England that he would become one of the best kings to sit on the English throne. This decent lad became a firm friend of Raleigh's, and visited him almost daily in the Tower.

"Only my father," said Henry scornfully, when speaking of Raleigh, "would keep such a bird in a cage."

It was for Henry that Raleigh set about writing his masterpiece, a *History of the World.* The first volume became another best seller when it was published. The boy loved history, and showed tremendous interest in the preparation of the great book.

Henry did everything he could to have Raleigh released from the Tower. He was just on the point of succeeding in 1612. James had agreed that Raleigh should be freed at Christmas time. But that November Prince Henry died, and James promptly broke his promise. In December "dwarf Cecil" also died, but Raleigh remained a prisoner.

During all those long years in the Tower, Raleigh never forgot Guiana. "I am sure," he wrote in letters to his friends, "that were I but free to go once more to the Orinoco, I could bring back a great store of gold."

The strange thing is that Raleigh was right about the presence of gold in that region. There are valuable gold mines today in Venezuela and also in British and French Guiana. But how Raleigh knew this remains a mystery.

The malevolent James still wanted to destroy Raleigh. For one thing the King was terrified at the thought of a fresh war with Spain. He was ready to do anything, however contemptible, to remain at peace with that country. It would please Spain greatly to know that Don Gualtero Rauli, as they called Raleigh, was dead. He was the one remaining English seaman whom they feared and hated.

For another thing, Raleigh was vastly more clever than James. The foolish King could not bear to have one of his disgraced subjects recognized as a many-sided genius by the leading scientists, historians, poets, and statesmen of Europe. In addition, the King loathed tobacco, and could never forgive Raleigh for having introduced it to England. All these reasons caused James to prepare one of the vilest plots in English history to bring about Raleigh's death.

He ordered Raleigh's release from the Tower in March, 1616, and then sent word to him. "You are free to go and search for gold in the Orinoco country," James declared. "But understand clearly that you must not injure any Spaniards you may chance to meet. Your life shall be forfeit should you take any Spanish lives."

Raleigh raked together just enough money to equip seven little vessels. In accordance with James's orders, he gave the King a list of these ships, details of the guns they carried,

the numbers of the crew, and the route he intended to follow.

The King, with horrible treachery, gave Raleigh's letter to Count Gondomar, the Spanish ambassador in England. Gondomar promptly sent it to Spain. In a covering letter to King Philip he wrote, "King James is very determined against Raleigh and will join with Your Majesty in ruining him. But King James desires that this plan be kept secret for some little while. Should the English people learn of it too soon, the matter might cause some stir amongst them."

Raleigh, now sixty-five years old, sailed for the Orinoco in August, 1617. He knew, perhaps, that he was gambling his life on the discovery of gold.

The fleet reached Trinidad after a wild and stormy voyage across the Atlantic. Raleigh remained with his ships, while five large boats, carrying 400 men, made the 200-mile journey up the Orinoco River. They were to head for a certain spot where two Indian gold mines were said to exist. In charge of these boats was honest Captain Keymis, an English university professor who had turned explorer and privateer captain.

"When you return you will find me here at Trinidad, dead or alive," Raleigh said to Keymis. "And if you do not find my ships here, you will find their ashes."

Spanish troops were, of course, waiting in ambush for the boats. Thanks to James's treachery, the Spanish king had been able to brief them in time. During the first encounter, five English and five Spaniards were killed. Among the English dead was Raleigh's twenty-three-year-old son, Walter. During the next four weeks there were fresh ambushes and more fighting. Twenty or thirty more Englishmen were slain. Some of those who were taken prisoner had their throats cut by the Spaniards. Raleigh's men fought only in self-defense. It was always the Spaniards who attacked them.

No one could carry on a search for gold along the river, while under fire from the jungle beside it. Keymis, sick at heart, gave the order to retreat. His sun-blistered boats, with their haggard and jungle-worn men, arrived back at Trinidad. Then he went to Raleigh's tent to make his report.

Poor Raleigh lost control of his temper. "You have ruined me utterly with the King!" he burst out. "Seeing that my own son was killed, I would not have cared if you had lost a hundred more lives in discovering the mines. At least that might have saved my reputation."

The faithful Keymis went back quietly to his own tent. There he committed suicide.

Among the items Keymis had brought back from the Orinoco was the actual report in Raleigh's own handwriting, which he had submitted to King James. It had been found in a Spanish officer's tent. Now Raleigh knew beyond all doubt that he had been deliberately betrayed by the royal renegade.

"A return to England will bring disaster to all of us," the senior officers said to Raleigh that evening. "Let us sail instead for Virginia and build our lives anew in a world of free men. We have the ships. We can earn a good living by plundering the Spanish galleons.

"I have long wanted to see Virginia with my own eyes," Raleigh replied quietly. "I believe it is the first of many English colonies that will arise in America. But, my friends, I will not have it said about me that I fled to escape punishment. We will sail directly to England."

Raleigh reached England in his own ship. The other vessels had deserted him to turn pirate in the West Indies. He was immediately placed under arrest, and the king of Spain was informed of it.

Even now Raleigh might have escaped, for both the French and Dutch would have welcomed this great old Elizabethan courtier, seaman, and poet. The governments of both countries had prepared careful plans, including ships and secret guides, by means of which he might have fled England. But Raleigh remained proud and fearless to the last. He refused to accept these kindly offers.

James's own wife, Anne, pleaded vainly with her royal husband to "deal sincerely and earnestly with Sir Walter Raleigh that his life may not be called in question."

But King Philip, through Count Gondomar, would allow no mercy to be shown toward Raleigh. England had sunk so low under ignoble King James that these Spaniards were able to order him harshly to arrange for the execution to take place. Raleigh, they said, had caused the deaths of many Spaniards; therefore, Raleigh must die. A hastily arranged English trial, as corrupt as the previous one, upheld King Philip's wishes. Raleigh was condemned to death.

On the last night of his life Raleigh turned to the Bible in his prison cell. On the flyleaf he wrote a poem.

Even such is time that takes in trust
Our youth, our joys, our all we have,

And pays us but with age and dust;
Who, in the dark and silent grave,
When we have wandered all our ways,
Shuts up the story of our days.
But from this earth, this grave, this dust,
The Lord shall raise me up, I trust.

The next morning, October 29, 1618, Raleigh walked calmly to the scaffold, and laid his head on the black oak execution block.

But the executioner had lost his nerve. Perhaps the man realized the great wrong he had been ordered to commit. He could not bring himself to raise the ax.

Raleigh snapped out his last command. "What dost thou fear? Strike, man, strike!"

The blade came down. For a moment the crowd stood in shocked and awed silence. Then, as their voices rose in angry confusion, a great shout rang out from somewhere in their midst. "We have not such another head in all England to be cut off."